Stories Around The Baby

By Robert A. Morgan

C.S.S. Publishing Company, Inc.
Lima, Ohio

STORIES AROUND THE BABY

Reprinted 1993

Library of Congress Cataloging-in-Publication Data

Morgan, Robert A., 1929-
Stories around the baby : sermons and children's lessons for Advent and Christmas / by Robert A. Morgan.
p. cm.
Includes index.
ISBN 1-55673-366-6
1. Advent sermons. 2. Christmas sermons. 3. Story sermons.
4. Children's sermons. 5. Presbyterian Church—Sermons.
6. Sermons, American. I. Title.
BV40.M67
252'.53—dc20 91-18223
CIP

9160 / ISBN 1-55673-366-6 PRINTED IN U.S.A.

This book is dedicated with abiding appreciation to the people of Westminster Presbyterian Church of Austin, my loyal companions in faith and fellowship for nearly twenty-five years.

RAM

Introduction

It will be clear to any reader of this book that some measure of "artistic license" has been taken by the author as he has unfolded these stories. Some aspects of the situations are presented which are beyond any information given to us in the Scriptures themselves. As far as I am aware, nothing has been included which in any way is contradicted in the Scriptures, or which contradicts the Scriptures. However, I trust the reader's imagination as much as my own — if the reader would in his own mind add other or different details to fill out the pictures, he is more than free to do so. I have filled them out in ways that seemed to me appropriate and faithful to the spirit of the stories.

RAM

Table of Contents

Advent 1 Sermon
Exodus 1:22—2:10

The Story Of The Rescued Baby

My name is Miriam. Perhaps you know me. You would be more familiar with my name if I had been born in another culture, for in other cultures the name "Miriam" is given as "Mary." But the way you would know me best, in any case, is through my brothers. I have two brothers. My brother, Aaron, is the leader of those who are priests for our people. And my brother Moses — well, you surely know my brother Moses. He is the leader of our people. If it were not for Moses, I think we would be no people at all. We would be slaves in Egypt, and we would by now be so deeply oppressed that there would be no hope of rediscovering our identity, let alone separating ourselves so that we could develop ourselves once more as a people, and become the people we understand that God means us to be. But that's a long story — a story which few persons but myself can any longer tell, because almost no one remembers it from the beginning, as I do. I'd like to tell you the story. To me, it's not only a fascinating story and a gripping story, but it's a story with so many overtones and undertones of meaning about our God, and about his plans and purposes for all his children.

Well, I said I remember the story from the beginning. Actually, I know it from even before the beginning. The story has a prelude from a time long before I was born, a time when our people were just one family, descendants of a man named Abraham and his wife Sarah. Abraham and Sarah had made a long journey to a special land our God had prepared for them. Our God promised Abraham that if Abraham would be faithful, he, our God, would be faithful to Abraham and Sarah, and not only to them but to all of their descendants, as many as grains of sand on the seashore, as many as stars in the sky. Abraham and Sarah had only one child, a son, Isaac. Isaac and his wife, Rebekah, had twin children, a son, Esau, and a son, Jacob, but the special promise of God was secured by Jacob. Jacob had 12 sons, so the family increased speedily then, and it was during a famine while Jacob and his family were living in Abraham's land that he and all of his sons decided to come to Egypt. Jacob's son, Joseph, had achieved a high position in the Egyptian government, and was able to obtain grain for food for his father and his brothers and their families, so they became settled and established in Egypt, and they prospered there for many years.

We're getting closer now to the beginning of my story, for my brothers and I are among those who descended from the children of Jacob, or Israel, as he came to be called later, after Jacob and his family had moved to Egypt. This Israelite family prospered wonderfully in Egypt, even during the time of the famine. And when plenty was restored, they prospered even more. But two things happened that changed life for them — for us — profoundly. We prospered so bountifully that the Egyptians began to see us not as a refugee-type family who needed help, but as an economic force which threatened them and their own interests. And beyond that, there were changes in the government as time went on, and the position of Jacob's son, Joseph, who from his position had been such a help and asset to our people, faded and was at last deliberately forgotten. The rulers of the Egyptians were called Pharaohs, and when the Pharaoh Ramses II came into power, it was a very bad day for us Israelites.

For Ramses said to his advisers, "We have to do something about these people. They are becoming more and mightier than we are!" And from that time on, our life in Egypt was changed. Ramses could simply have expelled us. He could have cast us out into the desert where at last we went, led by our God and by Moses. But he did not want to do that. Ramses wanted, as they say, "to have his cake and eat it too." He wanted to bring an end to the possibility that we could threaten the Egyptians by our numbers and our skills, but at the same time, he wanted to have our numbers and even some of our skills available for his own benefit and for the benefit of Egypt. He decided to put us to work in hard labor. He broke up our families, taking our men and young men into the construction service of Egypt. He even had our women making bricks, which he used in the building of great cities and great monuments. He made us help, in other words, to show what a great power Egypt was. The Egyptian taskmasters who were set over our people were cruel and kept us busy enough and separated enough so that the Egyptians felt sure we could neither organize in opposition to the government nor for an escape into the wilderness. Our people were angry and discouraged, but our God kept his promises to Abraham, and our God kept our people's spirits up so that they never lost their sense of who they were, nor their sense of relationship with one another and God.

In spite of the oppression, the hard labor we were put to and the efforts that the Pharaoh made to divide us from one another — in spite of all that, our people kept growing. It is written in one of the documents of those days, "The more they were oppressed, the more they multiplied and spread!" Pharaoh's plan was not working! He was getting labor out of us, but we were not submitting ourselves to him in spirit, nor were we losing our identity as a separate people and becoming the slave class that he wanted us to be. So his plans grew more severe. He determined that he had to start to kill us off selectively, and he directed that when Hebrew children were born, male children should be cast into the Nile River. Of course our people resisted this decree in every way they could. But with the overseers so much among us, it was hard to hide a baby very long — especially since the women as well as the men were often forced into slave labor.

We're at the point now where my own memory begins and takes over the story. My mother Jochabed was not only strong-willed, but she was very shrewd. My father Amram was, like all our Israelite men, in slavery to the Pharaoh, and all the men were in continual danger for their lives. Whenever the overseers saw any of the rules of Pharaoh being defied, the punishment was swift and utterly severe. There were more male babies destroyed than I can bear to think of, but it seemed to be a matter of letting the baby go or of the whole family being murdered. My mother, however, was not only hard to intimidate, but she was resourceful and wily. Mother had not been making bricks during the time just before my little brother was born, because she had been so weak and ill that she was no help to the crew. I had been pretty much in charge of things at home, which made it a little easier for us to keep the baby Moses unnoticed after he was born. Our neighbors were too involved with their own troubles to have gotten much involved in ours. We kept the baby hidden for nearly three months while all our family lived in constant dread. But Mother, always thoughtful, watched and waited for some opportunity, and finally it came.

Our little home — if such it could be called — was one of those nearest the Nile River, the very river into which male infants were supposed to be thrown. Not far down the river from our home there was a lovely little pool at the river's edge, surrounded by rushes so that it was private. Mother realized one day that the Pharaoh's daughter had discovered that pool and was coming often with her attendants to bathe. Mother developed a scheme in her mind, for she was beginning to realize that the baby Moses was growing to the point where we could no longer keep him hidden away. In fact, his strength and his beauty were the very things that would cause the attention of the authorities to be drawn to him and make him more vulnerable. Mother began to accumulate rushes from near the place in the river where the princess bathed and she started weaving them into the shape of a basket which looked like a little boat. We didn't know what was going on, but with my mother, one did not ask — one just waited and watched. Father was gone, laboring on a distant project of Pharaoh's. I was five or six years old then — at an age when I was not yet old enough or strong enough for overseers to take me away for labor, but old enough to do quite a bit for my mother. When the little boat which mother had made seemed large enough to her for the secret purpose she had in her mind, she took it down to the river and floated it out on the water. But it soon filled up and sank, much to her disappointment. Not discouraged for long, Mother brought it secretly back to our house and then began making trips in the dark of the night to the tar pit at the edge of the village, bringing home tar which she dabbed on the basket until it was covered outside. Again she tried it on the river, and this time it floated.

I could see that mother was both pleased about something and very distressed about something, but I did not know then what it was that was going on — I did not know that what had pleased her and what had distressed her were the same thing. She would hold the baby, looking at him with such love and such care that it sometimes frightened me. And then one afternoon she saw the princess coming to the river to bathe in the hidden pool. She wrapped my baby brother in his best cloth and she put him in the little basket she had made. As I watched, she took the basket with Moses down to the river and to the rushes at the edge of the pool. The rushes were thick and though Mother knew that the princess was in the pool, the princess could not see mother or the dark bundle Mother placed in the water. Mother made a sign to me to stay nearby.

Then she jiggled the basket so that Moses woke up, startled, and she pushed the basket into the reeds and the rushes. Moses was old enough by then to know that something strange was happening, and he began to cry. Mother had been careful with Moses, keeping the secret of his presence to ourselves, and one of the ways she'd been careful had been to keep him as much as possible from crying by holding him and rocking him in her arms. Moses was used to Mother's arms and Moses knew that whatever was rocking him now in his basket, was not our mother. As he began to cry more loudly, Mother did what must have been the hardest thing she had ever done in her life. She pushed Moses further into the rushes and hurried away, leaving only myself playing at the water's edge and watching. For all Mother knew, this was not only the end of her time of joy with Moses, but it had every possibility of being the end of our little baby's life. It was a gamble with the highest possible stakes.

The basket, with Moses now crying loudly, drifted deeper into the reeds, toward the women. I could not see everything that happened, but I could tell when the young women first began to be aware that there was a strange sound — a baby crying near them in the water. Then I saw the princess stand and point, and one of the attendants came in among the reeds and found the basket with our baby. I did not know whether to be happy or frightened, for Egyptian law then said that male Israelite babies should be put to death, and our baby was going into the hands of the princess of Egypt! But Mother had known exactly what she was doing. Mother had calculated about how Moses was such a beautiful baby that he would catch the interest of any young woman, and that is exactly what happened. I saw the basket being lifted out of the water and I saw the princess peer inside. I could hear Moses growing quieter as he sensed that the rocking of the river had stopped and that something new was happening. Soon, as I watched through the rushes, the princess was lifting Moses out of the basket and into her arms, and our baby was hushed as she held him. I heard her saying something to the young women with her about "this Israelite baby," and my heart nearly stopped.

But the princess seemed to be holding Moses protectively against her, and I understood then that this was exactly what Mother had planned for and hoped for.

Soon there was excited, even agitated conversation in the group, and I was bold enough to move on down the shore nearer the women. I could not understand all their words, but something — perhaps even our watchful God himself — led me to think that they were wondering what to do with a baby! I had then one of the brightest thoughts I've ever had — perhaps that thought, too, came from beyond me. For I thought, "Why don't I offer Mother to care for the baby!" I will never know whether the princess knew what was going on — somehow I've always thought it was too obvious not to be understood, but she never acknowledged a thing, nor even questioned why a child like myself happened to be so near at the very moment when, while she was bathing, a Hebrew baby floated into her pool. As soon as I made my suggestion of a Hebrew woman to care for the baby of the princess, the princess said, "Of course; go right now and get her." Mother could not believe it when I ran into the house, out of breath, and told her what she was supposed to do. Her plan had not included this!

But she came eagerly — almost so eagerly as to give the whole thing away. Yet there again, the princess showed no sign of understanding. She said simply, "Take this child and care for him. He is mine, and I will pay you for the care you give him. I will want to see him often, and when he is older, he will come and live with me." To Mother, that was not bad news, for she had wondered if she might be leaving Moses to the fate of sudden death, and instead, he would now have life and she would be part of it. I'm sure, as I look back, that Mother sensed the hand and the power of our God in this whole enterprise. Mother sensed even then that Moses was special in more ways than being our beautiful baby. Mother somehow understood that he must at all costs be cared for and protected.

All that was nearly a lifetime ago now, and I have neither the time nor the strength to tell you the rest of the story.

Perhaps you know some of it — how Moses grew up in Pharaoh's household but never forgot where he had come from; how he attacked and killed one day a particularly harsh Egyptian overseer of the Israelites, how he then fled to Midian and lived for many years in Midian until the day when our God met him in the wilderness and spoke to him out of the burning bush. Perhaps you know how Moses then returned to Egypt and took Aaron with him to Pharaoh to plead for the release of the Israelites. Pharaoh held out for a long time, but our God was on the side of my brothers, and at last Pharaoh said to Moses, "Take them and go!" Perhaps you know how the very sea waters parted under Moses' hand, so that we could escape from Egypt to the wilderness of Sinai. That was when I led the women, singing praise to God for our deliverance.

And I'm sure you know how long it's taken Moses to teach and train our people to grow from what they had been there at the last — just a crowd of slaves — and to become what God meant them to be, his people. It was those laws which my brother brought down from the mountain that seemed to be the one thing most necessary to our people's life together when at last they would get back to that land which Jacob and his children left so long ago. The time for that is nearly here now — I can tell. Our people at long last are nearly ready. I don't think I will get there, nor will my brother Aaron. Perhaps even Moses himself will not in the end get to that Promised Land — perhaps his work will have been done before that goal is reached.

That promise our God made to Abraham is a promise to everyone in all the world. The baby brother I helped rescue in the rushes, who became a leader in Egypt and became our people's leader is just part of God's larger plan and God's great purpose of delivering everyone, of making all people his people. I don't know how all this will happen, but I am so grateful that I've had a little part in all of it, and I'm more grateful that I've seen a little bit of what it means, and where it's going, and what will come! Amen.

Children's Lesson

What is at the very center of Christmas? *(Various answers — wait for "the baby," or "the baby Jesus.")*

Yes, the baby Jesus is at the very center of Christmas. He is the center of Christmas. All the music and the lights, the Christmas trees, the Christmas cards, the Christmas parties — these all come from the fact that God sent a special baby to earth on that first Christmas — a baby who grew up to be the Savior of all people.

But you know, Jesus was not the first baby whose coming was God's idea. In fact, I think every baby's coming is God's idea. I even think God has some special thing in mind for each of you, for all of us, to be and do, and that's why we each one are God's ideas.

But long before Jesus, there was a baby whom God seemed to look after very carefully. We're going to talk more about him this morning, but I want you to know his name and one or two things about him so that when we tell his story later, you will know what to listen for. His name was Moses. He was born in Egypt long ago. Little Hebrew babies born in Egypt at that time were in danger from soldiers. But Moses' mother and his sister — whose name was Miriam — were very clever. They made a floating boat and put the baby Moses in it so that he would float in the river to where the king's daughter was bathing. Moses' mother and Miriam knew that if the princess saw the baby, she would protect him.

And that's what happened. Not only that, but the princess decided to take him home with her and she asked Moses' mother to come along and look after him. Moses grew up in the king's palace, but when he was grown, he went back to his people, to the Hebrew people, and he led them out of Egypt and he taught them about God and showed them the great land where God had planned for them to live. Listen later, and I'll tell more of the story of the baby Moses.

Advent 2 Sermon
Numbers 22:1-30

The Story Of The Stubborn Donkey

Some people say that animals are dumb. I don't know exactly what "dumb" means. If it means not being perceptive, not being sensitive, not understanding, not caring, then people are wrong, for animals are perceptive and sensitive, they are understanding and caring. I know, because I am an animal, and I understand many things and I care a great deal. But if dumb means unable to speak with a human voice and in human words, which apparently it sometimes does mean, well then, animals may often be dumb. But not always, for I am an animal who finally had to speak, and speak in such a way that my human master could plainly understand me. I am a donkey — the donkey of a man who is a prophet. My master's name is Balaam, and we live in Mesopotamia, in a city named Pethor, near the Euphrates River. We live in that part of the world where human civilization began. I would tell you my own name if I had one, but I have never had a name. I am just Balaam's donkey.

But I can tell you my story — or better, our story. It's quite a story. Someone who has made a study of the stories in the Bible has called our story one of the most intriguing stories in the Old Testament, and at the end, it becomes clearly a story of what you know as Advent. But you can see all that for yourself as I tell you our story. And I am so glad that when I need it, I do have the power of speech, because that is what makes it possible for me to tell you all that happened when my master's services were sent for by the King of Moab.

I had been Balaam's donkey for several years before these particular events began to unfold — I had been Balaam's donkey long enough so that we knew each other's habits and expectations, and pretty much trusted each other. Donkeys are not elegant beasts, but we get the job done. The rich and powerful have camels especially for their longer journeys. Camels handle the mountain and desert terrain around here pretty well. Their dispositions aren't too good, but then we donkeys are seen often as being slow and stubborn, so we're in no position to be too judgmental. My life as Balaam's donkey had been ordinary before all these events about which I am going to tell you. I never foresaw or imagined what I'd be confronting, either.

I should tell you just a little about Balaam — you really don't need to know a lot. We live in this small city, somewhat out of the mainstream of traffic and life in our land, and Balaam generally goes about his business without pushing himself too hard and without making too many demands upon me. Balaam is what you might call a small-time wholesale merchant. He deals mostly in cloth, in dry goods — picking up odds and ends where he can, from caravans passing through and from weavers in our rural areas, and selling his goods to other merchants in our city. Balaam and I are on the move a good deal, but I don't mind that — it's better than being tethered all day in a stable. And I only have to carry Balaam — he has other donkeys who carry the goods.

But the more interesting side of Balaam's life is his hobby or special interest, or whatever you might call it, in magic —

not magic in the sense of making things or people disappear, or pulling rabbits out of hats, but magic in the sense of providing blessings and curses — for a price — to people who are in tight places and have tried everything else. It's those contacts Balaam has with the caravans which give him the chance to find out about many gods, and to pick up insights into the workings of the supernatural. People in our land have always been interested in the supernatural, in mysterious hidden powers and the possibility of finding and using them. I have to tell you I had not taken Balaam's interest in these things too seriously until that delegation arrived from the King of Moab. How on earth Balaam's name and reputation got as far as Moab, I cannot imagine — but then, as I said, he had these contacts with the caravans. And of course I was not where I could hear all that took place while I was tethered and he was off among strangers doing business in cloth, but also doing some business in magic.

Anyway, one day this impressive group of strangers arrived at the door of Balaam's small house. They said that they had been sent by King Balak of Moab, who had directed them to obtain the services of Balaam for the purpose of cursing an entire small nation of people. This was a larger order than Balaam had handled before, but he was very smooth in his responses as he obtained further information from the messengers. Their exact words were, "Balak is afraid that this people will lick up all the other nations in the region, just as an ox licks up all the grass in the field. These people have come out of Egypt, and if we don't slow them down, they are going to cover the face of the earth!" When Balaam heard "Egypt" a quick look of alarm passed over him, and he asked more specifically just who these objectional people were. "Why," said the messengers, "They call themselves the children of Israel." And the look on Balaam's face was one of more deep-seated alarm. But the messengers from Moab were so full of their subject that they did not perceive how Balaam was reacting. I was the one who knew how to read Balaam better than they did, for I have lived intimately with him for these years.

Balaam replied to the messengers, the "elders of Moab" as they called themselves, "I will not be able to tell you what I'm going to do for you until tomorrow." So the men went away, saying as they left, "Please try to come. Our King Balak is sure that whomever you bless will be blessed, and whomever you curse will be cursed!" They were hardly out of sight when Balaam and I started off for a visit with the people in a caravan which had come to our city two or three days earlier from the west from that very land of Egypt. Balaam knew enough about these children of Israel to know that he wanted to know more before he got involved with them, and he heard plenty in a short while from the members of that Egyptian caravan. He heard that the children of Israel had a special relationship with a powerful divinity, and that before they had left Egypt, they had instituted curses which involved locusts and flooding and epidemics, and at last the deaths of many male children.

I could see what was going on in Balaam's mind. He was attracted by the generous rewards the King of Moab had promised for his services, but he knew enough about the gods of the region and about their powers, that he did not want to take any chances getting on the wrong side of them. Most especially, he did not want to set himself against this god of Israel. We went back to Balaam's house, and that night, using his skills of incantation, Balaam tried to put himself in touch with the Israelite god. He connected with someone, anyway, and it seemed to him that the divinity he was communicating with said to him, "Who are these men who have been talking with you?" I think Balaam took it more as a test than as a request for information, but Balaam answered carefully, and then he seemed to hear the god's direction to him, "When these men come back, tell them you cannot go with them, for the people whom they want you to curse are being well blessed by me." For the moment, that was enough for Balaam, and he sent the elders back to King Balak with his refusal to serve.

But King Balak appeared to have his heart set on Balaam, for he sent a second delegation back to Pethor, made up of higher ranking elders, who offered Balaam a larger reward if he would only come and cast some kind of evil spell over those children of Israel. Balaam was strongly tempted, but thought he'd better have another conversation with the god, so this delegation also found some lodging and promised to return the next day. That night, Balaam seemed to hear the god direct him, saying, "You may go if you are bound to go, but you'd better be careful to say nothing over or about my Israelites except what I tell you to say!" On that basis, Balaam told the men the next day that he would go back with them, and as soon as we could get organized, Balaam and I were incorporated into their company.

But I think the god of those children of Israel would rather have had Balaam stay home — or else he wanted to impress upon him more fully the urgency of Balaam's saying only what this god would allow over the Israelites. In any case, we felt a certain supernatural tension in the atmosphere around us as our journey progressed, and it became visible just at the point where this story really becomes my story.

We were passing through an especially difficult and threatening portion of the route, a mountain area where some passages were very narrow, and where the footing was rather uncertain. I wasn't afraid. I haven't found a place yet that I cannot walk over or get through. But I could tell that Balaam was nervous. He had never been in such tight places — and I'm sure that the unsettled state of the spiritual atmosphere was affecting him, too. But it was myself who first got the big surprise. I was picking my way along the path when suddenly I saw a figure of tremendous brightness just in front of me, a man in white robes, glowing with unearthly sheen — a man who held a huge sword in his obviously strong right hand. He seemed to be pointing the sword straight at me and Balaam.

I stopped dead in my tracks, only to have Balaam beat me! Then I realized it was only I who was seeing the figure — Balaam saw nothing. I stumbled to the side, toward the wall of a vineyard that someone was trying to cultivate up in that lonely place. I lost my footing for a moment, and Balaam's leg was squeezed against the wall. This made him angrier, and he beat me again. I got my balance and tried to start forward, but the path by then had narrowed even more, and the angel filled the path from one side to the other, looking more threatening than ever. At this point, I simply lay down in the path, with Balaam on my back. I was careful not to tip him, but that was no help as far as his anger at me was concerned. He beat me for the third time, hard.

At that point, the most remarkable development occurred. Through all this time, thoughts had been going through my mind about what I would like to say to Balaam, if only I could talk to him in the language in which he was talking to me. And suddenly I found that very language rising in my throat. I felt that suddenly I was going to be able to say words. And when that feeling came upon me, it was no longer my anger at Balaam that I wanted to express, so much as my sorrow that he had not trusted me in the tight place where I could see what he could not, and I could walk where he could not. The words that came out were, "Balaam, am I not your faithful donkey, upon whom you have ridden every day of life? Have I ever let you down? Have I ever not been careful? Have I ever not been loyal to you?"

And it was as if, in the intensity of the moment, Balaam did not realize what an impossible thing had happened — that his donkey had talked to him. He simply heard my questions — they got through to him, through his preoccupation with the challenge of how to curse Israelites and stay in the framework their God had established. Balaam dropped his whip and sorrowfully replied to me, "No, you have never let me down." And at that moment, Balaam also was allowed to see the angel, and he nearly fell off my back in a faint. But he managed to hold onto himself enough so that what he actually did was to bow down and fall on his face before the angel. And the angel said to Balaam, "Why have you been beating your donkey? I have been trying to get your attention." And Balaam, thinking that the angel must be the god of the Israelites, declared, "You have my attention now. If you want me to go back home and forget this cursing project, I will certainly do that!'' But the angel said, ''No, you can go to Moab — only be sure to remember to say just the things that I tell you to say.'' Well, if Balaam had had any idea of double crossing that god of the Israelites, the encounter with the angel in the wilderness settled the issue once and for all.

I can tell you pretty speedily the rest of the story. We got to Moab, and Balak was eager to receive us and to put Balaam to work. Balaam warned Balak, ''The word that God puts in my mouth, that must I speak.'' King Balak took Balaam to the top of a high rise of ground overlooking some of the Israelites, and my master Balaam asked for seven altars to be built land seven bulls and seven rams for sacrifice. Balak did all that Balaam ordered, and the burnt offering was made, and King Balak and the elders and princes of Moab waited for Balaam's word of curse. But Balaam's word was, ''How can I curse those whom God has not cursed? How can I denounce those whom God has not denounced?'' And King Balak of Moab was very angry, but Balaam said simply, ''Must I not take heed to speak what the Lord puts into my mouth?''

King Balak thought he'd try again, and he took Balaam to another high place, to the top of Mount Pisgah and built seven more altars and offered more sacrifice. And again Balaam prophesied, and this time he declared, ''I have received a command to bless, for their god has blessed this people, and I cannot revoke or go against his blessing.'' And King Balak was more angry, and he said to Balaam, ''If you can't curse them, then at least don't take part in their blessing!'' And yet for a third time, Balak required Balaam to climb up a mountain, this time to Mount Peor, and again the altars were built and the bulls and rams were sacrificed, and this time, Balaam shouted out, ''How fair are your tents, oh Jacob, and your encampments, oh Israel. Jacob shalt eat up the nations his adversaries, and Israel shall break their bones in pieces.''

Well you can imagine how King Balak was filled with anger by this time. He struck his hands together and shouted at Balaam, ''I brought you here to curse my enemies, and three times you have blessed them! Go home!" But Balaam said, "I told you I would have to say what this god tells me to say, and there is even more that he is telling me to say now. He tells me to say that a star shall come out of Jacob, and a scepter shall rise out of Israel. And all the lands including Moab shall at last come under the rule of that star and that scepter!" Balak did not know what Balaam was talking about, but he knew he did not like it. It was clear that there would be no reward for Balaam after this, and he and I had to return to our home in Pethor by ourselves, after having been escorted so grandly to the land of Moab. But the trip back was not a bad journey. Somehow after that encounter with the angel in the wilderness, something had changed in Balaam. He seemed to trust me more — there was a better relationship between us. We got home safely, and compared with all that great adventure, our life has since been uneventful.

But I've thought a great deal about everything that happened then. I have not spoken much since I was given the gift of speech, but I have thought a good deal. Something bigger seemed to be going on in that pull-and-tug about Balaam cursing the Israelites for King Balak. It was really remarkable how those leaders of Moab heard about Balaam and came for him — who would have expected that my little prophet would play on such a large stage? And what is more remarkable is how he took direction from that strange god of the Israelites, even when it cost him the fee that Balak had promised. And then there's the matter of that angel in the road. I know I saw that angel far more clearly than Balaam did. My stopping before him simply strengthened my reputation as a stubborn donkey, but I knew what I was doing and why I had to do it. That god of the Israelites is really a powerful god, to have done something like that to us. He is the most powerful god Balaam, in all of his experiments and explorations in the spiritual ever has had anything to do with. I think one of the purposes of this whole episode was for that great God to show how he is not a god whose power is confined just to the Israelites. That God deals with everyone, including a poor foreign prophet like Balaam, and a poor foreign donkey like me.

And what was that about a scepter and a star? It doesn't really make sense, but since I have been able to speak, I have been hearing things as well. I have even been hearing other donkeys who use human speech, and I seem to hear them even when they are not here and now. The voice of one keeps somehow coming back to me — back as if it's way ahead of me in time, and yet as if we are somehow both part of the same enterprise:

"I," said the donkey, all shaggy and brown,
"I carried his mother up hill and down,
"I carried his mother to Bethlehem town,
"I," said the donkey, all shaggy and brown.

What donkey is that, and where and when? Whose mother? Where's Bethlehem? I don't know — I don't really know a thing. And yet I feel it's somehow all connected — Balaam going to work for the God of the Israelites, and my being warned and then befriended by an angel, and those words Balaam spoke about a scepter and a star. I'm sure that what that God had Balaam say is going to happen. Some special star is going to shine, some special thing is going to take place in a town called Bethlehem, and somehow, somehow, a donkey just like me is going to have a part in all of it. I wish I could be there — oh, how I wish I could be there. Amen.

Children's Lesson

Christmas has lots of animals in it, doesn't it? Can you tell me some animals that are connected to Christmas? *(Rudolph, reindeer, etc.)* Think about our creche, our manger scene — what animals are there? *(Sheep, cows, doves, camels, donkey.)* What did the donkey have to do with Christmas? *(Brought Mary to Bethlehem.)*

This morning I'm going to tell you about another donkey, a donkey who lived long before Mary's donkey — a donkey we can read about in the Bible, in the Old Testament. I don't know the name of this donkey, but his master's name was Balaam. This donkey, like Mary's donkey, was a good and faithful donkey — so faithful that one time he didn't do what Balaam wanted him to do. That may not sound like being a good donkey, but it was, because the donkey could see something Balaam could not see — an angel was blocking the way in front of Balaam and the donkey. Balaam grew angry and beat the donkey, and at that moment a most wonderful thing happened, for at that moment God gave the donkey the power to speak.

Sometimes we feel our animals and pets would like to speak to us. Well, Balaam's donkey said, "Balaam, why are you beating me? I've always looked after you and have always been faithful to you!" And Balaam was amazed — and just then he, too, could see the angel, who told Balaam and the donkey what God wanted them to do. In a few minutes I'll be telling more of the story of Balaam and his donkey. I think Balaam's donkey and Mary's donkey were actually a lot alike. Listen to the story and see if you don't think they were, too.

Advent 3 Sermon
Luke 19:1-10

The Story Of The Little Man Who Climbed A Tree

My name is Esther, and my husband is the chief tax collector in the city of Jericho. I'm sure you've heard of Jericho. You might know that it is one of the oldest cities in this land. It was a city long before our people came here. You remember — when they came from Egypt, the great signal to everyone living in this land was that the God of our people had helped them to capture the city of Jericho, by directing them what to do in order to cause the walls of Jericho to fall. Jericho was the key to the whole country. When Jericho was captured, everyone knew that this land belonged to our people.

And Jericho is such a lovely city. I never particularly enjoyed going up to Jerusalem, though that is the center of government, and it is looked upon as the symbolic center of our land. But Jerusalem seems new and almost bare, thrust up there on the hilltop, while Jericho nestles down in the lush valley, and receives the gentle breezes. Our palm trees and our gardens flourish, and the caravans pass through from east to west and west to east, letting their varieties of music fall upon our ears from places far and near. I love Jericho. I have never lived anywhere else, and I hope I never do.

But it's another matter whether Jericho loves me, and even more to the point, whether it loves my husband, Zacchaeus. Zacchaeus has a big responsibility. He is in charge of all the tax collecting in our city. The taxes he collects go to the Sanhedrin in Jerusalem, and to Rome. I have always been proud that my husband has a part in supporting the government of our land, and the magnificent power of Rome. Among many of our people, the Romans are very unpopular, but I look at it this way — if the Romans were not in authority over us, some other power would be, and I do not think we would be so well ordered, by so just a power. Ours is a very small land. Only rarely and briefly in our history have we been a free and independent people — and when we were, we could not even hold ourselves together, but became after King Solomon a kingdom divided, Israel and Judah. No wonder that after that, the Assyrians and Babylonians came in and plundered.

When the Persians took charge of the world, they gave us some order. And then there were the Greeks, and now the Romans. From what I can see, we are about as well off as we can be now, for though Rome takes some taxes us from us, Rome gives us our lives otherwise to live as we wish. We maintain our own patterns of commerce, and we carry out our own religious rituals. We keep our culture intact, thanks, I'd say to Rome! If ever the anti-Romans become dominant among us, that's when things will be bad for our people. I know, women do not usually seem to think about this sort of thing, but I think. Maybe even my name has something to do with that. The great Esther was queen in the time of the Persians. She thought carefully, and saved our people from destruction. I will never save our people, but I do believe it's important for one to think about things like this, to have one's own opinions and judgments and not merely accept whatever is the popular mood of the moment.

And it's surely a good thing that I am as independent as I am in judgment, or else the general feeling of the people about tax collectors could ruin my life. I do not understand all the technicalities of my husband's business. I do not believe that that is my role, my business. My role is to be Zacchaeus' wife, to make and keep this home for which he so well provides, and to give him my love and my loyalty in answer to the love and loyalty which he so faithfully gives me. It would have been my role as well to direct the upbringing of our children, but we have not been blessed with children, which has been a matter of quiet pain to both of us. Yet sometimes I think that our loyalty to each other is, if anything, the more intense because we have only each other.

I said that I do not know all the details of my husband's business, but I know enough — and this is probably the greatest burden that I carry, that we carry — I know enough to know that there do not exist clear rules and laws about collecting taxes. That sounds strange when I have said how well ordered the Roman authority is. But that's one of the principles of its ordering, that it does not establish all the details of the system. The Romans simply let it be known what is important to them, and in the area of tax collecting, what is important is the minimum amount of tax that they require. How the funds should be obtained, they do not in detail direct. How much the local government may extract from the taxing system, how much the Sanhedrin in Jerusalem may demand — the Romans don't specify. Nor is there any standard about compensation for the tax collectors themselves. As far as I know, Zacchaeus himself does not even have a firm agreement with the men who work for him in Jericho about their own share of the taxes. They know what they must give him, and the difference between that and what they collect is their share. It's their responsibility to keep the people content enough so that the tax collecting process can continue to go smoothly. Zacchaeus has in some ways the most difficult position in the system because he depends upon those who work for him, but he never knows when some Roman or Jewish official will demand more than

Zacchaeus expected to have to provide. Zacchaeus is in the middle, and if he were not so wise and so smooth, life for him and for us both would be a great deal harder.

As it is, we are not poor. We are able to live in considerable comfort. But we are not popular, for no one is ever satisfied that the tax is being fair to him. I've thought that if there ever is a significant rebellion against Roman power, it will be because of resentment at the tax system. I've wished the Romans could help us to work out a system more specific and fair, but I suppose that such a thing as that is impossible from so far away as Rome, and for so many different peoples as Rome now is administering. I tell you all this just to tell you how life is with us, where we are and who we are. And I chiefly tell you all this so that you may understand the beauty and the wonder of the great experience that Zacchaeus had, that we both had, with the new teacher Jesus when he passed through Jericho not long ago, on his way to Jerusalem. I sometimes think our lives will never be the same — it was that wonderful, that overwhelming an experience.

I don't think I had heard before about this Jesus, though it's strangely hard to remember what I knew and didn't know before he came. Zacchaeus apparently had heard enough about him to want to get a look at him. It seems that this Jesus had been unusually thoughtful of tax collectors. Having met him myself, I'd say now that he is unusually thoughtful of tax collectors and everyone else. But Zacchaeus knew that Jesus had not only eaten a meal more than once with tax collectors up in Galilee, which has for a long time been a socially unacceptable thing to do in our land — Jesus had not only eaten meals more than once with tax collectors, but he had invited the chief tax collector of Capernaum to become one of his close friends, or "disciples," as they seem to be called. Tax collectors have for so long been shunned by the so-called respectable group that it was a bold thing for Jesus to be in touch with them, let alone to bring one of them into his intimate circle.

In any case, Zacchaeus knew enough about this that when he heard the other day that Jesus was expected to be passing through Jericho, Zacchaeus decided he wanted to see him. Zacchaeus inquired when Jesus was expected, and he learned that Jesus was just outside the city. Jesus was apparently on his way to Jerusalem and would not be stopping in Jericho. Zacchaeus closed his office and hurried toward the north gate, where the main road from Galilee and Samaria enters the city to go through it. Zacchaeus found quite a crowd gathered, waiting for Jesus. Now a crowd does not willingly open itself up for my husband, the tax collector, and besides that, Zacchaeus is short, like myself, and always has a hard time seeing what is going on. But Zacchaeus has always been resourceful and agile. He had to develop those qualities in order to make up for being short, and those qualities have helped him to become successful in many things.

When Zacchaeus saw the crowd, he knew there was no point in his waiting at the edge of the crowd, because he would never see anything. But his eye fell on that old sycamore tree near the gate, and he concluded that that was the answer to his problem. He gave a few coins to a boy with a donkey and asked the boy to take the donkey to the tree so that he could stand on its back and reach the lowest branch. In that way, Zacchaeus climbed up into the tree, and had apparently just gotten himself into position when he heard some kind of commotion outside the gate. We learned afterward that old Bartimaeus, the blind beggar who has taken his position there at the gate each day for so many years, had recovered his eyesight as Jesus was coming into the city, and it caused a great stir. There were two or three of Jesus' special friends with Jesus, and by the time they all got to the gate, they had picked up a number of curiosity seekers from near Jericho, so that Jesus came into the city surrounded by quite a group. And then there was the crowd waiting inside the gate as Jesus and the crowd around him came into the city. If Zacchaeus had not been up in that tree, he would never have been able to see anything!

And I guess we will never know whether it was his being up in the tree that drew the attention of Jesus to him, but it must have been that, and Jesus must have said to those nearby, "Who is that fellow up in the sycamore tree?" And someone must have replied, "Oh, him — that's Zacchaeus the tax collector!" In any case, the most remarkable thing happened, for Jesus looked up into the sycamore tree and cried out, "Zacchaeus, come down from that tree! I'm going to rest at your house today and have a meal with you if you are willing." Zacchaeus was so stunned that it apparently took him a few moments to gather his wits and come down and you can imagine how startled the crowd was. I think at first they were pleased that Jesus seemed to know one of them, and that he was going to stay in Jericho after all, but then when they realized who it was that he had recognized, and who it was that he was going to visit, their mood changed, and they grew angry and resentful. Zacchaeus of course was used to that mood, that reaction. But this time he did something about it, something that astounded the crowd and himself! The people of Jericho have not forgotten yet, and I believe they will think differently of Zacchaeus for a long while. But I think it was partly because he wanted no bad reflection from himself to fall on Jesus after Jesus had so graciously recognized him. Zacchaeus shouted out for all to hear, "Lord, half of my goods I will give to the poor, and if I have cheated any individual, I'll make it up to him four times!" The crowd was dumbstruck, but Zacchaeus meant what he said, and he has since figured carefully what our wealth is, and has begun to distribute to the needy what he calculates to be half of our savings. As far as the cheating part goes, there's been no more honest man at work in this whole tax collecting enterprise than my husband, so few if any could truly charge that Zacchaeus had cheated them. But Zacchaeus knows what the feelings of the people are, and this was his chance to put the burden of truth upon them. As far as I know, no one has come forth to make a claim against him. And as for half of our savings, I have seen no evidence so far that our standard of living will change much. As I told you, Zacchaeus and myself are wealthy — so wealthy that to give up half of what we have still leaves us not uncomfortable.

What a change all this has made in our relationships with people here in Jericho! Whether it was Jesus choosing our house to stay in for a few brief hours, or Zacchaeus' declaration prompted by Jesus' call to him, I do not know. But we are shunned no longer. People acknowledge us in the street. Other women speak to me in the market. Our servants seem proud and not surly and grudging about the fact that they work in our home. For the first time ever, we have been summoned to the great banquet held every year by the leading merchants of Jericho. The pattern of our lives has been transformed by the events of that brief day — we live in reconciliation with our fellow citizens now.

And something has changed within ourselves, as well. To tell you the truth, I can hardly remember any of the conversation between Jesus and ourselves while he was with us. When the messenger arrived from Zacchaeus telling me to get ready for a special guest for supper, I was startled — we so rarely have guests. And the time Jesus was with us seemed to fly by while I was busy with the food and serving. Of course we entertained as well as those friends of his who had come with him from Galilee — I think they were named Peter, and James, and John. They said that others of their group had gone on earlier to Jerusalem, and still others were yet to come from Galilee. This trip to Jerusalem seemed to be important to them all, and I could not tell whether they were looking forward to it or were fearful about it. We have not heard from any of them since they left us and went on. No doubt we will hear something sooner or later.

But it was not what Jesus said that made a difference in our lives — just that he was here in our home. His very presence seemed to bless us and to change us. I know I have been happier since he was here than I had ever been in my life — happier and more content. It is not just that we live in a different relationship with others now. It's that we live in a different relationship even with God. I cannot explain it — I just know that what I am saying is true.

And I must tell you about the amazing conversation I had with a strange woman at the market yesterday. As I said, people greet us now who never before acknowledged us in any way, so I was not totally surprised when this young woman approached me and said, "I believe you're Esther, and your husband is Zacchaeus the tax collector. Jesus of Nazareth was in your home the other day. My name is Mary. I grew up in Bethlehem, and my father is an innkeeper there. When I was a little girl, during the time of the great census, we, too, had some special visitors. A man named Joseph and his wife Mary wanted a room in our inn. The inn was full, but my father could see that Joseph's wife was just about to have a baby, and he offered the barn. That very night their baby was born in our barn, and it was the strangest and most wonderful thing how everyone knew about it and wanted to see that baby. The Bethlehem villagers came, shepherds from the nearby countryside came, even some foreign noblemen with a rich looking camel train came. They all wanted to see that baby. That baby grew up to be Jesus of Nazareth. His parents returned to Nazareth not long after he was born, and we lost all track of him until recently when we began to hear stories about him and his teaching and travels. I heard about Zacchaeus wanting so much to see Jesus that he climbed the sycamore tree, and it reminded me of how the doves had come into the barn and sat in the rafters looking down at that baby! No one who saw Jesus when he was a baby ever forgot the experience. Somehow, just seeing him seemed to change their lives. I wish that I had seen him when he was in Jericho. How wonderful it must have been for you to have him in your home. I can imagine you'll never forget it!"

I appreciated so much Mary telling me her story that I asked her to come home with me and tell Zacchaeus, too. She did. I think we have a new friend there. And when she told Zacchaeus about how they all had come to see the baby in the barn, Zacchaeus' eyes filled with tears so moving was her story, and so close was it to his original experience of wanting to see Jesus.

And all this has been my story, and there is no more now, but if ever you should have the chance to see Jesus, then, oh, you must see him! You will never know such joy as when you see him, and your very heart will be changed and made new when you have seen him! Amen.

Children's Lesson

Do you ever get tired of being smaller than grownups? I think every child has that feeling sometimes. But children can look forward to growing bigger. It might be harder if one were already grown up and was short in comparison with other people. There was a man once who wanted very badly to see Jesus, but he was short, and there was a big crowd around Jesus, and this man had to figure out a way to get himself above the crowd so that he could see over the heads of the other people. Do you have any idea what he might have done?

He climbed a tree. And much to his surprise and to the surprise of everyone else, Jesus saw him up in that tree and called him down. Zacchaeus was the man's name. Jesus called out, "Zacchaeus, come down from that tree!" And if that wasn't a big enough surprise, Jesus added, "I'm calling you down because I'm going to have supper in your house tonight." Well, this was a thrill far beyond anything Zacchaeus had hoped for — and it changed his whole life. I'm going to be telling more of the story of Zacchaeus in a few minutes. Listen and see what happened when Jesus announced before the whole crowd that he would have dinner at the house of Zacchaeus.

Advent 4 Sermon
John 11:1-15

The Story Of The Man Who Lived Again

Our home is a simple home, and we are a simple family. I have never understood what it is about us that has drawn so many friends to us — friends not only from our own village, but from Jerusalem and elsewhere. Perhaps it's our simplicity. We do not live elaborate lives — we could not afford to. But we care for people. We enjoy being in touch with what's going on in our world and our time. We always are glad to be in touch with what is going on with our people. I think our people have a special gift for the religious side of life — not that that means the same thing to all of us.

Take our family, for instance — there is a wide difference among us as to what religion is. To my sister Martha, it is a matter of being busy, doing good things. Martha is always busy. She gets so much done. There's always a hubbub around her. I think she is one of the reasons why we have so many friends. Martha is always animated in energetic hospitality.

I've thought recently that to some extent, Martha's chief religious activity is entertaining our friends, bringing people of many kinds together to discuss current events and especially current religious events, and to enjoy the food, the fellowship of one another and the small comforts of our home. Our home itself is small, but that also may be why people like to be here. There is an intimacy about being here that the grand homes of many of our friends, especially those in Jerusalem, simply cannot achieve.

And that says something about my kind of religious interests. Martha likes to be busy, doing things for people, bringing them together, serving them, making it possible for them to share their feelings and their insights in good fellowship. Myself, I love to have guests and to be among them — not so much to participate as to watch and to listen. My religion seems to express itself best, to be most active, as I listen, watch and ponder, meditate, think over what I hear and what new understandings have come to me. I listen to this rabbi, to that priest, to that devoted temple worshiper, to this good friend. I have no gifts for preparing a feast, but I love to be in the company of those who come to our home, just to be there and hear them as they talk with one another about our people's heritage, about what the world is like today, about what it means to have the Romans here, and about what the new teachers are saying.

But probably the greatest attraction of our home is our brother Lazarus. Lazarus is a wonderful host, as well as a wonderful brother. He has a way of welcoming everyone and fitting each one smoothly into whatever group is here without placing himself at the center of attention. It may take some people a short while to realize, that so much of their pleasure in being with us is because of Lazarus. Lazarus has a way of putting people at ease without their realizing what is hapening. He had a way of drawing them out into the group just at the points where they best fit in. Lazarus really cares about people. He cares for each one as the person each one is. I believe that when people are in our home, they discover things about themselves that they had not known, and they often express themseves in ways that had not occurred to them before. Of course I know Lazarus better than any of them, and I know how thoughtfully he handles people. But even those who are new to our circle soon develop an appreciation and affection for Lazarus.

And of course the friendship between Lazarus and Jesus is very special. I used to wonder at the fact that Jesus never asked Lazarus to be one of the friends in that group that seemed nearly always to be with him, but Jesus probably understood that Lazarus was so loyal to his sisters and so necessary to our home that he could not have left us even for the sake of accompanying Jesus. And Jesus may have felt too that it was necessary to himself for our home to remain intact as a place of refuge and refreshment for him, that he needed to have Lazarus here for his own sake. We were so pleased to have Jesus feel that our home was valuable to him, and we enjoyed deeply the times he came to us and spent with us.

When I think back, I think how little we realized the importance of what was going on that first time Jesus came. We were having guests in — the usual kind of guests, assembled from our village in Jerusalem. They were talking, as I remember, about how the religious habits of the Pharisees agreed with our traditions from Moses, and how the Pharisees differed from Moses. Someone said, "The new teacher from Galilee is in town — I wonder what he thinks about this matter." And Lazarus, always eager to make such times as rich as possible, said, "I think I'll go to him and ask him to join us." Lazarus went to invite Jesus to our home, and Jesus responded very rapidly. Now that I know him so well, it does not surprise me, because it always meant a great deal to Jesus to be in touch with such groups as those that gathered in our home. Jesus was always glad to share viewpoints about issues of contemporary life, and he was always eager to be in touch with people. We had a wonderful evening with him that first time, and something must have satisfied him, too, because he was our friend from then on. He seemed to appreciate each one of us for special reasons, as well as enjoying the three of us together. He understood Martha in her busy serving. He understood my quiet interest in ideas and people, and especially in him. Perhaps best of all, he understood Lazarus and cared for him. And that of course was the point at which our most wonderful experience with Jesus occurred.

There was a strange sickness in Judea during those months. I couldn't call it an epidemic, because it was not that widespread. Nor was it like those plagues in which all members of a family are swept away. It would find just one individual person here and another there. But once a person had been touched by the illness, he and all his family could know that he would be dead very soon. None of our medicines or skills seemed to have any effect. You can imagine that when Lazarus began to be ill, we were in terror, for it was impossible to our thinking that our brother Lazarus might die. If Lazarus were to die, we felt, then we would want to die, too. That was the kind of family we were.

And of course it was Martha who had the idea of sending for Jesus. Jesus was up in Galilee then, but he was by that time well enough known that one could track him down in any part of our land — some people always seemed to know where Jesus was. Martha sent one of the young men from our village up to Galilee to find Jesus and tell him that Lazarus was ill. I don't know what Martha expected Jesus to do. If all the healers in Jerusalem had no cure for Lazarus' illness, it seemed unlikely that our friend Jesus could no anything but weep with us for him. And I really think that's all that Martha expected, then — she simply wanted Jesus to share in our love and our grief for Lazarus. She paid the boy no small sum to find Jesus, and we did our best to care for Lazarus.

But our worst fears became fact, for the course of the illness with Lazarus was unusually swift, and we could see that he would not live much longer. I think Lazarus knew as well as we did how ill he was, but in his gentleness, he expressed nothing but gratitude for our care, and appeared to trust that all would be well. But Lazarus died even before the young man got back from Galilee. Our messenger assured us that he had delivered our message to Jesus, but in our grief we hardly were aware of his return. Our many friends were wonderful, even though their pain and sense of loss were hard for them to bear as well. We observed all the proper rituals for death. Lazarus' body was washed and bound, and before sunset that day it was buried in our family's burying place just at the edge of our village. When the heavy stone was replaced, I felt almost as if it were myself from whom the light of life was being cut off. We carried out the customary three days' mourning as if we were under some kind of a spell. And secretly, within our deepest hearts, we had somehow begun to feel that if Jesus had been with us, Lazarus might not have died. Our own hope, I think, did not die altogether until the three days of the mourning time had passed, and we had had no word from Jesus. I don't know exactly what we expected, for Lazarus was, after all, dead.

But Jesus had not failed to take our message seriously. We heard the strange story later from others. I wondered at first why our young messenger had not told us of Jesus' response to the word about Lazarus, but I see now that that young messenger never considered the message to be anything more than the usual words of concern — the "Tell them I hope he will be well soon" sort of thing. But what Jesus had actually said when the message reached him was, "The illness of Lazarus will not result in his death. Its purpose instead is the glory of God." Of course, the messenger could not have told us those words — they would have seemed cruel, in view of the fact that Lazarus was obviously dying.

And then, we understood, instead of setting out to come to us as soon as possible, Jesus purposely lingered in Galilee until he felt sure that Lazarus had died. In any case, his disciples would have tried to prevent Jesus from coming down here, because by then Jesus was in deep disfavor among the religious authorities because of his teachings, and there had even been threats that he would be executed if he ever came back to Judea. But at length Jesus told the disciples not that Lazarus had died, but that he had fallen asleep. They took this for a good sign, as is the case of that illness which seemed to come to a crisis, and when the crisis is reached, the sick person either dies or relaxes and his fever passes and he falls into a deep and restful sleep. The disciples said to Jesus, "Wonderful! If he has fallen asleep, then he will recover." So Jesus had to make it plain to them, "Lazarus is dead." But then he said, so strangely, "I'm glad that I was not there, but let us go to him now." And his disciples believed that Jesus' coming to us would be not only Jesus' response to Lazarus' death, but his stepping out to meet his own death as well. Of course, both of these beliefs were true, but how little we all understood, even then — even now.

Jesus reached the outskirts of Bethany on the fourth day after Lazarus' death and burial. Though the initial period of mourning was over, many of our friends were still with us. The fact that we lived so near to Jerusalem means that they were able to come back each day and still return to their own homes at night. Of course, Jesus' coming was being noticed — many knew that Martha had sent to tell him Lazarus was ill, and some had already expressed their surprise and disappointment that we had not heard from him. Someone came in to tell us that Jesus was nearing the village. We both were deeply touched, and yet his reaching us then almost seemed to make us feel more keenly our disappointment that he had not been with us before Lazarus died. In any case, Martha, always the busy one, went straight out to meet Jesus. I remained at home with our guests.

Martha told me later that she could not help herself, that the first thing she said when she met Jesus in the way was, "Lord, if you had come sooner, perhaps Lazarus would not have died." That was not a very warm welcome, but Martha has always been one to say what she feels, and at that point, that's what both of us were feeling. Jesus said to her, "Lazarus is going to rise." Martha was well enough informed about religious viewpoints to know that some of the Pharisees had taught for many years about a resurrection at the end of time, when all the dead would once again be made alive. She said to Jesus that she was willing to believe Lazarus might be resurrected at the last day, but that that was no great comfort now. Then Jesus spoke to her in new words about himself. Looking back, we see that he was telling her what he was going to do, as well as who he was. She did not understand it all then, but she understood some, for when Jesus said to her, "I am the Resurrection and the Life. Do you believe this?" Martha replied, "You are the Christ, the Son of God!" Now we had heard often about the Christ, God's special son who would be sent for the redemption of the world. That was a matter often talked about in our home, by our guests. But none of us, not even Martha or myself, had ever dreamed before that Jesus might be that Christ. Later, we understood that we were not the first to develop that perception — Peter, Jesus' disciple, had expressed it to Jesus on behalf of several of the disciples: "You are the Christ, the Son of the living God!"

But even then, Martha had no idea of what Jesus planned to do. She simply left Jesus and came to get me, in the hope that I might have a little time with him before he joined the crowd at our home. But they all sensed something, for when Jesus told me that Jesus had come and wanted to see me, many of them went out with me to where Jesus was waiting for me. When I saw him, I simply dropped at his feet in gratitude that he had come, but even I could not help but express my disappointment that he had come too late. Jesus seemed very much moved by a grief of his own as I was there sharing my grief with him. Jesus asked me to take him to Lazarus' tomb. There again, Jesus wept for Lazarus. Whomever else Jesus was, he was a deeply caring man who loved his friends.

But when Jesus directed that the great stone at the entrance to the tomb should be moved out of the way, that was too much for Martha. She thought that for some reason Jesus wanted to see Lazarus' body, and she knew that by the fourth day it would not be fit to view. But Jesus insisted, and much to our consternation, the men, with great effort, moved away the stone. Then Jesus did not go to the tomb. Instead, he prayed, and after that called out to Lazarus, "Come here!" We thought that Jesus had lost his reason — and in one way of course, he had. Jesus was acting out of some depth or height in himself that was far, far beyond his human reason. Jesus called out, "Lazarus, come here," and I was so awestruck by Jesus' cry that somehow I was not surprised when Lazarus appeared, with all the grave cloths still around him. It was such an incredible moment that there was not a sound in the whole crowd — we all were struck dumb. Then the moment passed, and Jesus looked at Lazarus and all the rest of us as if to say, "Don't you know what to do? Take away those grave cloths, for he is not dead! Then let the man go home."

It's strange, but the experience was so awesome that no one could speak. Lazarus went to the house, and when we next saw him, he was himself and recovered, and neither he nor we have made a reference since to any of it. Jesus went on to Jerusalem, and soon after, those things his disciples had feared most of all took place. He was arrested, tried briefly, and crucified. We were still in such awe of the thing he did for us that we somehow could not think seriously about what was happening to him, and when the report came to us that within three days after his death, Jesus was back with his disciples, our reaction was. "Of course. If Lazarus is back with us, then Jesus is back with them. Did he not say to Martha that he was himself the Resurrection and the Life?" We never saw Jesus again, but we did not need to. From that time on, it was as if he was continually with us. The power of his presence, which had overwhelmed us there at Lazarus' tomb, somehow remained, and it no longer mattered to us who lived or died, because we felt that life with Jesus, life in Jesus, was beyond time and above death. I have never talked to Lazarus about how it was for him in death, in the tomb. Somehow I've felt that that no longer matters. All that matters is the life which we all have in Jesus.

But I have thought of one thing since we learned of Jesus' own death. He who dies has had to have been born. And though I know very little about Jesus' birth, I think that, next to his conquering death both for Lazarus and himself, the other great moment with Jesus must have been the time when he was born. Someone told me once that he was born in Bethlehem, not far away from here, and that his mother's name was Mary, like my own. The world did not know then, I realize, what had happened, who had come. But what a sense of life and light there must have been! The very heavens must have shone — it could not have been otherwise.

For Jesus could have been no other one than God himself among us here. No other one but God himself can turn death into life and leave us with a sense of life that can't be touched by death. What glory came with him! It was the great experience of my life to be here when Jesus called Lazarus out of the tomb. But what a wonderful thing it also must have been when Jesus was born. What a wonderful thing it would have been to be there when Jesus came into this world, into our life there at Bethlehem! Amen.

Children's Lesson

At Christmas time, we're thinking about Jesus' birth. What is the name of the time when we think about the death of Jesus, and especially about what happened after Jesus' death? *(Easter . . .)*

Christmas and Easter seem in some ways very far apart. Jesus was 33 years old at the time of his death, so they were 33 years apart in time. And birth and death usually seem far apart in mood and spirit, too. Birth is a happy time — death is a sad time. But there was great happiness soon after Jesus' death — do you remember why?

In fact, it's hard to associate death with Jesus. From the time when he was born on that first Christmas night, it was life that was associated with Jesus. Jesus taught time after time that all of us should be concerned with life, not death. Jesus' gift to all of us is life — it is his Christmas present and his present forever.

Once when one of Jesus' closest friends, whose name was Lazarus, died, Jesus showed how life is important and not death. Jesus went to where Lazarus' body had been buried several days before, in a cave, and he called, "Lazarus — come here!" And Lazarus, who had been dead for several days, was suddenly alive again, and he came out to Jesus and to his family and friends. I'm going to tell more of the story of Jesus and Lazarus in a few minutes. As you listen, you can remember how the best gift of Christmas, of Jesus, is life!

Christmas Sermon
Matthew 1:18-25

The Greatest Story Ever Told Or Heard

The opening verses of the gospel of Matthew, through the 17th verse, provide the passage of Scripture which is often known as the "begats," tracing the genealogy of Jesus Christ from Abraham to Joseph. The chapter begins: "The book of the generation of Jesus Christ, the son of David, the sonof Abraham." Forty-two generations later, the 16th verse reads, "And Jacob begat Joseph the husband of Mary, of whom was born Jesus, who is called Christ." Beginning at verse 18, the chapter reads: "Now the birth of Jesus the Messiah took place in this way. When his mother Mary had been engaged to Joseph, but before they lived together, she was found to be with child from the Holy Spirit. Her husband Joseph, being a righteous man and unwilling to expose her to public disgrace, planned to dismiss her quietly. But just when he had resolved to do this, an angel of the Lord appeared to him in a dream and said, 'Joseph, son of David, do not be afraid to take

Mary as your wife, for the child conceived in her is from the Holy Spirit. She will bear a son, and you are to name him Jesus, for he will save his people from their sins.' All this took place to fulfill what had been spoken by the Lord through the prophet: 'Look, the virgin shall conceive and bear a son, and they shall name him Emmanuel,' which means, 'God is with us.' When Joseph awoke from sleep, he did as the angel of the Lord commanded him; he took her as his wife, but had no marital relations with her until she had borne a son; and he named him Jesus."

Tonight we are going to imagine that Joseph is telling his story. Whoever tells this story tells the greatest story ever told. Whoever hears this story hears the greatest story ever heard!

I am getting old. I know it's time, and inescapable this time. I felt I was getting old once before, but Mary changed all that. She came into my life and it was just as if she gave me a new life, a second life. I had been lonely for so long! When my wife Suzannah died, and our baby died with her, I felt my life too had ended. All the joy seemed gone and all the brightness was made dark. There was nothing but my work, my craft of wood. Working the wood seemed for so long to be the only meaning. And I must say, beautiful things came out of that wood when I worked it with my hands. They were things I made to be useful, but they had a beauty in them, too, which was the only beauty my heart knew, for the long years after Suzannah died before I found my Mary.

I'm not good with words, not fluent or artistic with words. But there are things that should be made known about the life of Mary and myself. I have to tell the story as best I can, not just because it is our story, but because it's an important story. I could say that it began when I went to work on the addition to the house of Caleb of Capernaum. Caleb was growing wealthy. He wanted his home to reflect more of his wealth, and he wanted me to add some great rooms to it. I was glad for the work, not only because that kind of work was my life, but because it was also my living. There was another reason for me to be glad for the work at Caleb's. That was Mary. But I didn't know about Mary when Caleb first came to me. I only knew that there was work — my kind of work, and work which would last quite a while.

I said that the story began when I went to work for Caleb, but in a way it began long before — it began perhaps when the business of my grandfather who lived in Bethlehem began to spread to other cities, and he sent my father here to Galilee, to Nazareth. Or perhaps the story began earlier than that. Who knows? In any case, it was well that I didn't become a trader like my father and my grandfather, for when my grandfather died, the heart of the network was gone, and my father and brothers had a hard time making their living here. I had my hands, my skill in carpentry, and there seemed always something waiting for me to do. But Bethlehem is a part of the story, and I will explain to you soon where it fits in.

I met Mary soon after I went to work for Caleb. She served me my noon meals. Her mother was the cook at Caleb's, and her father kept the stables. Mary was young, but self-possessed — quiet and kind and gentle, yet aware of everything. At first I thought the feelings I began to have toward her were nothing but the foolish imaginations of an old man. Then I thought, "If she were only closer to my age, I do believe a new life could begin for me with her." And then I started to perceive that there was something more than duty in her watchfulness of me, her attention to me and my needs as I worked. I spoke quietly with her father about her, and he knew already — she herself had told her father that if I should ever tell him that I cared for her, she would be willing to become my wife.

My heart was full of feelings that I thought had long since gone. Mary and I had happy visits about what our life together would be when my work for Caleb was done and we would return, husband and wife, to my home in Nazareth. Then that troubling shadow fell upon us. I overheard the whisperings of other servants one day, and that very afternoon, before I could bring up the matter with him, Mary's father came to me in deep distress and said, "We do not understand it. Mary's going to have a baby. We know you and she have never been together as husband and wife. She will not tell us any more. She says that she must talk with you. Undoubtedly you will want us to put her away now. Undoubtedly this will bring to an end any plans that you and she had made together.'' I was hurt and even more than that, I was confused. Things like this happened with other young women, but I could not believe it about Mary. She had said she wanted to talk with me. I wanted to talk with her, but not then. Something in me could not deal with the matter right then. I told her father that I could make no decision about Mary and myself until I had talked with her, but that I was not ready then to talk with her. He seemed to understand. I went back to my work, but my mind and my heart were all in turmoil.

That night as I tossed on my bed, I felt also that I must be dreaming, for before me suddenly an angel stood, more glorious a sight than my eyes had ever seen. The angel knew what was consuming me, for without any introductory words he said to me, ''Joseph, don't be afraid to take Mary as your wife. It's true that she is going to have a child, but the child has been conceived in her by the Holy Spirit. The child will be a son, and you will name him Jesus because he will save the people from their sins. And he will also be known as Emmanuel, for men will say, 'In Jesus God is with us.' ''

Suddenly the brightness was no longer of an angel, but it was the brightness of the dawn. I got up and ran to the kitchen where Mary might be. I found her, took her by the hand, and took her with me into Caleb's little back garden. There I held her in my arms, and there she told me what was in her heart. ''Joseph,'' she said, ''this will seem very strange, and I do not myself know what to make of it. An angel came to me, and declared that God had found me good. He told me I was going to have a baby, a son whom I should call Jesus, who would be a king. I was afraid, and I said to the angel, 'This cannot be, for I have never known a man.' The angel simply said, 'The power of God will do this to you, and the baby who will be born will be called the Son of God!' ''

I knew then that Mary would be my wife, and that we both would be the parents of this special child. My heart was filled again with joy — so much so that I wanted Mary to be mine right then. But my work for Caleb was not quite finished, and Mary felt she needed to go to visit her cousin Elizabeth before she was married. We agreed to be married when she returned, and I gave myself joyfully to the completion of the work for Caleb.

But a new development occurred which seemed to make life difficult again for us. A decree came from Rome about an unusual census which was to be made in our land, and in which each man was required to enroll himself in his ancestral city. For most people, that was no great thing, because most people lived where their fathers before them had lived. But as I told you, my father had come from Bethlehem, and this decree meant that I had to go back to enroll myself there in Bethlehem soon. Mary returned from Elizabeth's just as I finished the work at Caleb's home. We were married immediately, but instead of going to Nazareth together, we set out on the journey to Bethlehem. It was unthinkable for me to leave Mary at a time like this in her life. My plan was to get down to Bethlehem and back before the baby was born. But it was a slow and a difficult journey. An unusually large number of people seemed to be traveling, probably due in part to the census. Accommodations at night were crowded and poor, and the weather was cold. I was so fearful for my Mary. I remembered again how everything had gone at a similar time with my Suzannah. But Mary kept assuring me that all was well, and that all would be well.

We finally reached Bethlehem, but it had been clear to me for some time that we would not get back to Nazareth before the baby was born, and I had begun to be afraid that we might not even reach Bethlehem before that time. In Bethlehem, I went immediately to the old inn. The innkeeper's father had known my grandfather and my uncles well. I told him our situation and he was completely sympathetic. But he said, "There's not even a corner available here in the inn, and in any case, this crowded inn is no place for a woman in the condition of your wife. You would be better off in the stable." At first, I thought he was using some expression of speech, but then I realized he was serious. He meant to put us up in the stable. Mary was so uncomplaining, and as it turned out, the innkeeper had done us a great favor. The stable was warm and private. The animals were far better company than most of the guests in the inn would have been. There was clean soft straw, and the innkeeper provided for as many of our needs as possible. We were almost more comfortable there than we had been since leaving Nazareth.

That very night the baby was born. Mary and I handled things alone. Considering the trip and all, the birth went remarkably well, and I had mercifully little time to think about Suzannah and my earlier experience with birth. Neither did we have much time to think of all we had been told about the baby. In any case, I was so grateful that we were in Bethlehem, where we could stay a little while. Mary and I were both in awe of the baby. He was a lovely baby. Even the animals seemed hushed around us, and seemed to be looking in wonder at all that was happening there in their barn. When it was over, and Mary had wrapped the baby, she laid him in the manger straw, and they both went to sleep. I went outdoors to breathe the night air deeply, and it was a night I shall never forget. The radiance of the sky was glorious, and one star especially seemed almost to be overhead and shining down on the very place where we were. I thought of the things we had been told about our baby then, and where he had come from, and what he was going to be and to do. It almost seemed to me that that star was God's sign, pointing down, saying, "Here he is — this baby who will be known as my son!"

But the baby is my son, as well. No one else knows about the angel visitors whom Mary and I had. She didn't even tell her parents. When they saw that in spite of her pregnancy I was planning to marry her, they asked no questions and never remarked again about these circumstances. They gave her to me with their blessing. And since we had to set out for

Bethlehem so soon after we were married, and did not return until the baby was no longer an infant, no one else had any reason to raise questions. Jesus is taken simply as our son.

More happened at Bethlehem. Of course I enrolled for the census as I had to. But more happened, I mean, with the baby. A group of nearby shepherds came just after dawn the morning after he was born, to tell us that an angel chorus had appeared to them when they were out during the night in the fields with their sheep. They were told not to be afraid, but to rejoice because a Savior had been born to them that very night in Bethlehem. And they were told that if they went looking for the baby, they would find him in a manger. The shepherds were nearly as moved as we when they told us their story while they gazed down on our baby. And a few days afterward, an almost more impressive delegation came — three Oriental noblemen who looked quite out of place there at the inn barn, but they, too, had come to worship the new king.

Shortly afterward we were warned that we must go on to Egypt, that the baby was in danger, that all babies were in danger from King Herod. We were used to traveling by then, and in some ways it was easier for Mary than before the baby was born. We did not return to Nazareth for some while, but when we did get back, our lives developed a happy and comfortable order. Jesus has not been difficult to bring up, certainly no more so than any other child. He has learned my trade and does it well, and the people of our city seem to trust him and respect him to the measure that they would trust and respect any young man. We had a troublesome and even frightening time a year ago when we took Jesus to Jerusalem at Passover. We lost him, and it was several days before someone reported to us that he was in the temple, talking with the scribes. Mary spoke sharply to him when at last we found him, but with a strange gentleness — almost an aloofness — he said to us, "I must be about my father's business," and we knew then that it was not myself to whom he was referring.

Now, as I said, I'm truly an old man. Mary, still young, still lovely, will not have me with her a great deal longer.

But Mary has Jesus, and now he is grown enough to care for her and to provide for her. I have no knowledge yet of what those prophecies meant which were given to us before he was born. I may not ever know — I may not ever see them fulfilled. But I still believe them, I still trust them. So many little things have told us that this is a special child. Ever since that night of Jesus' birth, I have remembered what my own heart said and what the shepherds said, as well as what the angels had said earlier to Mary and myself. I have remembered what an incredibly beautiful sight that night sky was. I have remembered how the very animals stood there in awe. Truly, the night of Jesus' birth confirmed for us beyond all doubt the truth of what we had been told. Whoever this boy is, he is a blessing.

And my part in his life has not been small, and I am grateful, grateful that I could be part of it and so grateful for him. I always took pride in my craftsmanship, the works of my hands, but this boy will be the most beautiful thing upon which I have set my hand. Sometimes I see a shadow on his face, sometimes I know deep things are going on within his heart. All that, I'll never understand. But I do know enough so that when death comes for me I will die content. Through this child God has blessed us. In this child, God will bless all hearts! Amen.

Children's Lesson

So many people could tell us wonderful stories about the night when Jesus was born. Surely the innkeeper who provided the little family a space in his barn must have had a wonderful story to tell. I imagined once the story of the innkeeper's daughter told years later to her own small children about the night when a very special baby was born in her father's barn. And think of the stories the animals who shared that barn could tell! We know something about the story the shepherds would have told — of being visited in the middle of the night by angels, and of how they found the baby and his parents in the stable. We know something about the story the wise men would have told about the long journey they made because they saw a star that gave a message to them and then about how they found the baby at last and gave him their gift.

The story the baby's mother would have told would have been a wonderful story. We know something about it, at least about how the angel came to her and told her she was going to be the mother of God's Son. But no less wonderful would have been the story which Joseph, Jesus' father, would have told. In a few minutes I'm going to tell that story as I have imagined Joseph might have told it. Joseph was not a young man, you know, when Jesus was born. He was quite a bit older than most of your fathers. He had seen a lot of life, and he had had a lot of sorrow. But what a wonderful thing it was for him that he could have the happiness and joy of being Jesus' father. Be ready to listen when I tell you some of what that experience might have meant to Joseph.